Momentous Materials

Concrete

by Trudy Becker

FOCUS
READERS®

BEACON

www.focusreaders.com

Focus Readers is distributed by North Star Editions:
sales@northstareditions.com | 888-417-0195

Produced for Focus Readers by Red Line Editorial.

Photographs ©: Shutterstock Images, cover, 1, 4, 7, 8, 10, 13, 14, 16, 19, 22, 24, 26, 29; iStockphoto, 20–21

Library of Congress Cataloging-in-Publication Data
Names: Becker, Trudy, author.
Title: Concrete / by Trudy Becker.
Description: Mendota Heights, MN : Focus Readers, [2024] | Series:
  Momentous materials | Includes bibliographical references and index. |
  Audience: Grades 2-3
Identifiers: LCCN 2023031234 (print) | LCCN 2023031235 (ebook) | ISBN
  9798889980308 (hardcover) | ISBN 9798889980735 (paperback) | ISBN
  9798889981558 (ebook pdf) | ISBN 9798889981169 (hosted ebook)
Subjects: LCSH: Concrete--Juvenile literature.
Classification: LCC TA439 .B363 2024 (print) | LCC TA439 (ebook) | DDC
  620.1/36--dc23/eng/20230706
LC record available at https://lccn.loc.gov/2023031234
LC ebook record available at https://lccn.loc.gov/2023031235

Printed in the United States of America
Mankato, MN
012024

About the Author

Trudy Becker lives in Minneapolis, Minnesota. She likes exploring new places and loves anything involving books.

Table of Contents

CHAPTER 1

Strong and Lasting 5

CHAPTER 2

History of Concrete 9

CHAPTER 3

Modern Methods 15

 THAT'S AMAZING!

Ready-Mix 20

CHAPTER 4

A Concrete World 23

Focus on Concrete • 28

Glossary • 30

To Learn More • 31

Index • 32

Strong and Lasting

Students in Nevada are on a field trip. Their bus pulls up to Hoover **Dam**. When the students get out, they see a huge structure. Its gray surface stretches as far as they can see.

Hoover Dam is on the border between Nevada and Arizona.

The tour guide tells them about the dam. He says it is made of concrete. Concrete is a common building material. It is very strong and hard. The material can support the dam's whole weight. It can hold back the water. It can also handle years and years of weather.

Did You Know?

The world's largest concrete structure is the Three Gorges Dam. It is in China.

 Concrete helps make roads strong so they can support heavy vehicles.

When the tour is done, the class leaves. They drive back to school. The road is made of concrete. Their school is made of concrete, too. This amazing material is all around.

Chapter 2

History of Concrete

Humans started using early forms of concrete long ago. In the Middle East, ancient people used **mortar**. They built stone houses. When the mortar dried, it held the stones together.

 Ancient Egyptians used mortar to hold together the stones that form the pyramids.

 The Pantheon is an ancient building in Rome, Italy. It has the world's largest concrete dome.

The ancient Romans added ash to their mortar. The ash made a stronger concrete. This improvement helped the Romans build huge structures.

The Roman Empire ended in the 400s CE. Some of their methods for making concrete were lost. After that, people still used mortar. But it was not as strong as Roman concrete.

Scientists started making improvements in the late 1700s. The biggest change came in 1824. That was when Joseph Aspdin invented Portland **cement**. Cement is a key ingredient of concrete. Aspdin made cement in a new way.

He used a carefully measured mix of **lime** and clay. It worked much better than other mixes.

In the 1900s, concrete production grew quickly. People used it to build the modern world. For instance, they built skyscrapers. They also built smooth, long-lasting roads.

Did You Know?

Portland cement was named after the Isle of Portland. This island is in England. It has stones that look similar to cement.

 Concrete is a common material in skyscrapers.

However, all that concrete led to problems. Producing concrete releases **greenhouse gases**. These gases are causing **climate change**. Scientists warn that concrete production must change.

Chapter 3

Modern Methods

Concrete has four basic parts. They are sand, gravel, water, and cement. Cement is what **binds** concrete together. It makes the concrete strong. It also gives concrete its gray color.

 Concrete has to dry for about two days before people can walk on it.

 Mixing less water into the cement can make concrete stronger.

Cement starts from crushed limestone. The crushed stone is heated in a **kiln**. Then, it is ground into powder. After that, the powder is mixed with water. That makes a thick paste.

Next, sand and gravel are added to the paste. **Admixtures** are also added. The ancient Romans used admixtures such as milk, blood, and animal fat. But today, people use chemicals. Admixtures give concrete different traits. For example, some make concrete harden faster. Others make concrete more waterproof.

The basic steps of producing concrete have not changed much since ancient times. However, technology has improved. For example, older kilns did not move. But modern kilns spin slowly. This movement helps mix the cement evenly. It helps control the temperature, too.

Did You Know?

Modern cement kilns can be 500 feet (152 m) long.

 Kilns usually rotate three to five times per minute.

Scientists are still finding ways to improve concrete. In 1998, they invented a concrete made from recycled materials. And in 2006, scientists made a concrete that can repair its own cracks.

Ready-Mix

Good timing is important when building with concrete. Concrete must be mixed and poured at the right moment. Otherwise, the parts could separate. Or the concrete could harden too early.

In the past, workers made concrete at building sites. They poured the concrete right after making it. But in 1913, ready-mix concrete was created. This concrete is made ahead of time. People load it into trucks that have mixers. The mixers keep turning. That way, the concrete does not harden. Workers can use it later.

Today, three-fourths of all concrete is ready-mix.

Chapter 4

A Concrete World

Concrete is a huge part of today's world. For example, roads and bridges are often made from concrete. So are sidewalks and driveways. But one of concrete's most common uses is hard to see.

 Concrete bridges can support the weight of many vehicles.

 Concrete can boost temperatures in cities by as much as 22 degrees Fahrenheit (12°C).

Concrete is used in foundations. It supports the weight of buildings. Concrete is very useful. But it also causes several problems. In cities, concrete covers much of the ground. So, there is less ground to soak up rain. That can make floods worse.

Also, concrete traps heat. So, many people use air conditioners to stay cool. These machines run on electricity. Most electricity is made by burning fossil fuels.

Did You Know?

Water is the only substance that humans use more than concrete.

 Approximately seven out of ten people in the world live in buildings made with concrete.

The production of concrete also creates problems. That's because most kilns are heated with fossil fuels. Concrete production causes up to 8 percent of all greenhouse gases.

More concrete structures are being built every year. These structures could make climate change even worse. However, scientists are trying to fix these problems.

Some scientists are creating new ways to heat kilns. They want to do it without fossil fuels. Others hope to make concrete that can absorb large amounts of greenhouse gases. That could make up for the amount released during production.

FOCUS ON
Concrete

Write your answers on a separate piece of paper.

1. Write a paragraph explaining the main ideas of Chapter 4.

2. Do you think people should keep using concrete even though it harms the environment? Why or why not?

3. When was ready-mix concrete invented?
   - **A.** 1913
   - **B.** 1998
   - **C.** 2006

4. What invention could help reduce floods in cities?
   - **A.** concrete that repairs its own cracks
   - **B.** concrete made from recycled materials
   - **C.** concrete that lets water soak through

5. What does **traits** mean in this book?

*Admixtures give concrete different **traits**. For example, some make concrete harden faster. Others make concrete more waterproof.*

    A. materials that are difficult to break

    B. details that make something different

    C. workers who build concrete towers

6. What does **foundations** mean in this book?

*Concrete is used in **foundations**. It supports the weight of buildings.*

    A. the newest parts of buildings

    B. the highest parts of buildings

    C. the bottom parts of buildings

Answer key on page 32.

Glossary

admixtures
Ingredients that are added to a mixture.

binds
Makes things stick together.

cement
A powdery material that can be mixed with other things to form concrete.

climate change
A human-caused global crisis involving long-term changes in Earth's temperature and weather patterns.

dam
A wall that stops water from flowing.

greenhouse gases
Gases that trap heat in Earth's atmosphere, causing climate change.

kiln
An oven that hardens or dries out materials.

lime
A material made by heating limestone or chalk and then adding water.

mortar
A material that holds bricks or stones together.

To Learn More

BOOKS

Henzel, Cynthia Kennedy. *Redesigning Cities to Fight Climate Change*. Mendota Heights, MN: Focus Readers, 2023.

Theule, Larissa. *Concrete: From the Ground Up*. Somerville, MA: Candlewick Press, 2022.

Yasuda, Anita. *Exploring Hoover Dam*. Mendota Heights, MN: Focus Readers, 2020.

NOTE TO EDUCATORS

Visit **www.focusreaders.com** to find lesson plans, activities, links, and other resources related to this title.

Index

A
admixtures, 17
Aspdin, Joseph, 11–12

C
cement, 11–12, 15–16

F
fossil fuels, 25–27
foundations, 24

G
gravel, 15, 17
greenhouse gases, 13, 26–27

H
Hoover Dam, 5–6

K
kilns, 16, 18, 26–27

M
Middle East, 9
mixers, 20
mortar, 9–11

P
Portland cement, 11–12

R
ready-mix concrete, 20
roads, 7, 12, 23
Romans, 10–11, 17

S
sand, 15, 17

T
Three Gorges Dam, 6